Himeji Castle

by Grace Hansen

Abdo Kids Jumbo is an Imprint of Abdo Kids
abdobooks.com

abdobooks.com

Published by Abdo Kids, a division of ABDO, P.O. Box 398166, Minneapolis, Minnesota 55439.

Printed in the United States of America, North Mankato, Minnesota.

052021

092021

Photo Credits: Alamy, Getty Images, iStock, Shutterstock

Production Contributors: Teddy Borth, Jennie Forsberg, Grace Hansen
Design Contributors: Candice Keimig, Pakou Moua

Library of Congress Control Number: 2020947579

Publisher's Cataloging-in-Publication Data

Names: Hansen, Grace, author.

Title: Himeji castle / by Grace Hansen

Description: Minneapolis, Minnesota : Abdo Kids, 2022 | Series: Famous castles | Includes online resources and index.

Identifiers: ISBN 9781098207304 (lib. bdg.) | ISBN 9781098208141 (ebook) | ISBN 9781098208561 (Read-to-Me ebook)

Subjects: LCSH: Himejijō (Himeji-shi, Japan)--Juvenile literature. | Castles--Juvenile literature. | Architecture--Juvenile literature.

Classification: DDC 728.81--dc23

Table of Contents

A Samurai Fortress

Before there was a castle on Himeyama Hill in Japan, there was a fortress. In the early 1300s, **samurai** built a fort. It was meant for military purposes.

Asia
Japan
Himeji

During the **Middle Ages**, walls and other defenses were built around the fort. Over the years, the protections grew larger and more complicated. Still today, it is easy to get lost on the grounds.

Tenshu on the Hill

In time, the fort was taken down. A castle was built in its place. In 1581, military leader Toyotomi Hideyoshi built a ***tenshu*** to go along with the other buildings.

Toyotomi Hideyoshi

Between 1601 and 1609, Ikeda Terumasa did a lot of work at Himeji. Ikeda was a ***daimyo*** in the **feudal system**. He built the ***tenshu*** even taller.

Ikeda Terumasa

Honda Tadamasa was a ***daimyo*** of Himeji beginning in 1617. He added many buildings to the grounds.

Honda Tadamasa

One building Honda added was a special tower. It was for his daughter-in-law, Princess Sen. She is one of the most famous people to live at Himeji.

Princess Sen

Many ***daimyos*** lived in the castle throughout the years. Each left their mark. But in 1871, the **feudal system** of Japan ended. It was up to a new form of government to protect the castle.

Over the years, Himeji Castle survived destruction, wars, and earthquakes. The castle became a **UNESCO** World Heritage site in 1993. In 2010, **restoration** work began.

Himeji Today

The castle reopened to visitors in 2015. Himeji is the most visited and beautiful castle in Japan. Tourists can see everything from historic weapons to more than 1,000 cherry trees.

More Facts

- At the top of the castle are *shachihoko*, or tigerfish. It is believed that the creature can bring rain. Because Himeji is made of wood and plaster, the tigerfish protect the castle from fire.

- Himeji Castle is sometimes called White Egret Castle or White Heron Castle. Some people believe the castle looks like a bird about to take flight.

- In 1601, control of Himeji Castle was given to Ikeda Terumasa as a reward. He had just been a commander in a very important Japanese feudal battle. Much of what Terumasa did to the castle is what we see today.

Glossary

daimyo – in feudal Japan, any of the great lords who were very powerful landholders. They were beneath shoguns (chief military commanders) in society.

feudal system – or feudalism, a political and economic system in Japan during the Middle Ages. Royal or noble families owned land and allowed people to live on and farm the land in exchange for military service and loyalty.

Middle Ages – a period in history that lasted from about 500 to about 1500 CE. Something relating to the Middle Ages is medieval.

restoration – a return to an original form or condition.

samurai – a warrior in the service of a lord in medieval Japan. They were beneath *daimyos* and above peasants in society.

tenshu – the central tower or main keep of a Japanese castle. It is the castle's most defining feature.

UNESCO – short for the United Nations Educational, Scientific, and Cultural Organization, an agency that brings countries together in education, science, and culture.

Index